PROVINCETOWN POETS SERIES
first books by new poets

VOLUME VII
David Matias
Fifth Season

VOLUME VI
Ellen Dudley
Slow Burn

VOLUME V
Mairym Cruz-Bernal
On Her Face the Light of La Luna

VOLUME IV
Martha Rhodes
At the Gate

VOLUME III
Anne-Marie Levine
Euphorbia

VOLUME II
Michael Klein
1990

VOLUME I
Keith Althaus
Rival Heavens

EUPHORBIA

PROVINCETOWN POETS, VOLUME III
Series Editor: Christopher Busa

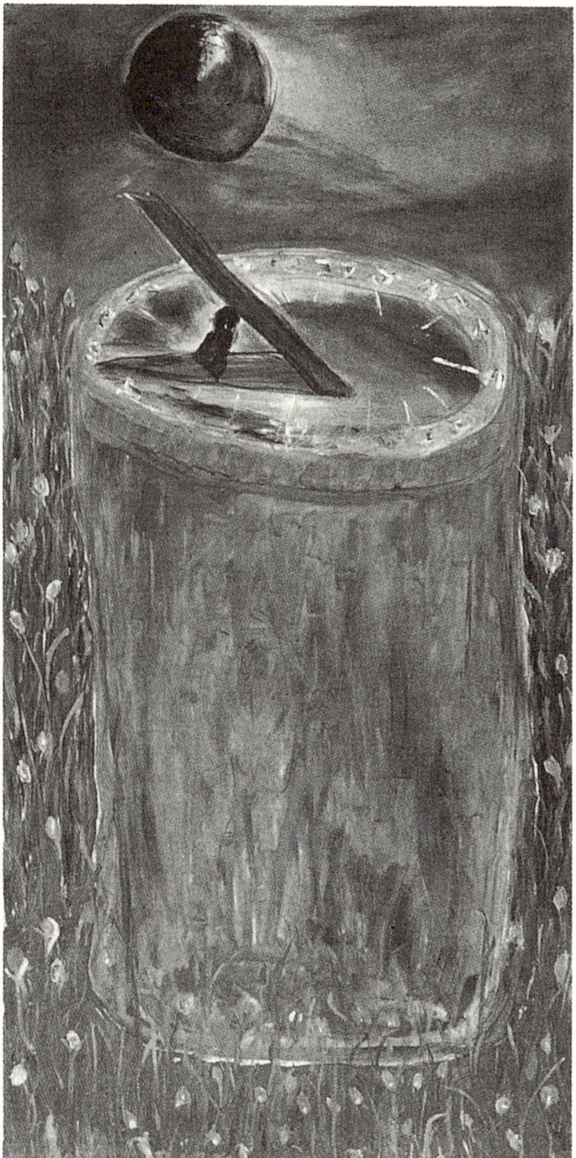

EUPHORBIA

by Anne-Marie Levine

PROVINCETOWN ARTS PRESS

ACKNOWLEDGMENTS

Grateful acknowledgment is made to the following periodicals where some of these poems, at times in earlier versions, first appeared: *The Beloit Poetry Journal, The New York Quarterly, The New York Times, Parnassus, Pequod, Ploughshares, Provincetown Arts,* and *Sojourner.*

The quotation on page 45 is from *Remembering Poets* by Donald Hall. The quotation on page 47 is from Count Harry Kessler, 1933.

I wish to thank the New York Foundation for the Arts for support during the writing of this book.

Thanks also to Barbara Burn for expert advice at the last minute; to Elise Asher, who always made me laugh and more than that; to Bill for inhabiting the poems; to David Levine for reading and rereading the poems, and for invaluable criticism, friendship, and support. Most of all, love and thanks to my guide, Stanley Kunitz.

This book is funded in part by the Massachusetts Cultural Council, a state agency that also receives support from the National Endowment for the Arts.

© 1994 by Anne-Marie Levine. All rights reserved. No part of this book may be used or reproduced in any manner without written permission except in the case of brief quotations embodied in critical articles and reviews.

For information write to Provincetown Arts Press, Inc.
650 Commercial Street, Provincetown, MA 02657

FIRST EDITION – 2ND PRINTING 1999

Designed by Gillian Drake
Frontispiece: Elise Asher

PAPER   ISBN 0-944854-11-7
CLOTH   ISBN 0-944854-12-5

Library of Congress Catalog Card Number: 94-065401

Printed in USA

CONTENTS

I

From a Movieland Childhood	PAGE 13
Kinderszenen	15
smallpoems	18
Snakes Do It	19
Ghosts	20
Piano Lesson	26
Words for the Poet	28
Soup	29

II

Singles	37
Night's Bodies	38
Telegram	40
Hoist with Her Own Petard	41
Return to the Poem	42
Two-Part Invention	43
Yours	48
Euphorbia	49
Brown Study	50
Novena	51

III

Nun of My Dreams	55
Variations	59
Sad about Cora DuBois	61
A Toe Fantasy	66
Friends	68
Autobiographical Poetry	70

EUPHORBIA

I

FROM A MOVIELAND CHILDHOOD

Stopped at a red light in Beverly Hills   Donald O'Connor
and Robert Wagner in their cars on either side of me talking
to each other across my open convertible

Running into Dorothy Lamour on Beverly Drive   shocked at her
pitted and marked skin   the result of years of movie makeup
I was told

Invited with my friend Brenda by her director father to a movie
set where Virginia Mayo and Turhan Bey were filming   We
had our pictures taken with them just the four of us   I still
remember Brenda's phone number   Crestview 5-2421
I called her every Saturday

Cynthia Hirsch always had Margaret O'Brien to her birthday parties

My father was a member of Hillcrest the golf club of the Jewish
comedians   the Marx Brothers the Ritz Brothers George Burns
George Jessel Jack Benny
My father Sylvain had a FrenchGermanFlemishPolish accent
They called him Tex

The California of my nostalgia is sun and ocean
Everything else was carefully cultivated
Year-round green grass watered by a buried sprinkler
system every evening   an abundance of flowers and flowering
bushes planted and tended by Japanese gardeners   hibiscus
camellia gardenia fuchsia begonia mimosa snapdragon
The best memories are of night-blooming jasmine and early-morning
hummingbirds over the honeysuckle bushes outside my window
I never saw a weed

Beverly Hills was a quiet village then
No Gucci no Pucci no foreigners   just us locals wandering
around in shorts and jeans long before the rest of the world
caught on to our comfortable ways

Now I run into soap-opera stars on Manhattan streets
They look at me to see if I recognize them
Our stars didn't do that

KINDERSZENEN

1.
A giant palm tree marked the house   Flora and I would lie by
the side of the kidney-shaped swimming pool dropping seedless
green grapes into our mouths while my springer spaniel from one
of Jerry Lewis's litters chased shadows about the garden   She
was liver-and-white and had a pedigree   Calla lilies and
Shasta daisies, tended by our Belgian cook, Gaby, lolled in the
flower beds next to Mrs. Meinecke's house   Her given name was
Bird and her husband's Ferd   On the other side, Mrs. Regnier's
mimosa tree cast a giant shadow that became a dragon every night
in the corner of my room when the light was extinguished   I
dreamt then of witches or of colored choo-choo trains that crossed
a blue ocean to Europe

2.
I read *Photoplay* and *Modern Screen* and Maurois's biography of
Disraeli   I appropriated young Benjamin's motto, "Learn not
for pleasure but for action," though I could not have told what
actions I was preparing   I read Archie and Wonder Woman comic
books, and Christopher Fry's verse play *A Phoenix Too Frequent*
     "Nothing but the harmless day gone into black is all the dark
is, and so what's my trouble . . ."   I knew great chunks of it,
Doto's lines, by heart   I followed the adventures of Cherry Ames
and Sue Barton, student nurses, and the poems of Dylan Thomas kept
me awake at night   I studied the dialogues of Plato because I
thought philosophy might provide answers to my profound but inchoate
questions   When I won the Book Week awards at school they gave
me a children's book called *Downright Dencey* for a prize

3.
There was oil everywhere   on the property of the Hillcrest
Country Club where my father played golf   where the return
on their oil rights paid the members' dues   on the Beverly
Hills High School land where I attended school   where a man
working high up on the oil rig was shot in the neck by a member
of the girls' archery team   I was good at archery   At college
I had an archery professor whose doctoral dissertation correlated
girls' archery scores with their menstrual cycles   She read it
to us on rainy days   on fine days she liked to put her heavy
arms about me, body pressed against my back, to show me the proper
form

4.
We were asked to memorize a poem upon graduation from the eighth
grade at the El Rodeo School   We recited, from Sir Walter Scott's
"Lay of the Last Minstrel":   "Breathes there the man with soul
so dead,   Who never to himself hath said,   This is my own, my
native land!   Whose heart hath ne'er within him burned   As home
his footsteps he hath turned   From wandering on a foreign strand!
    If such there breathe, go, mark him well;   For him no minstrel
raptures swell. . . ."

5.
Arnold Schoenberg died in Los Angeles, having failed to produce
viable movie music   Many great musicians lived there in the
days of the Second World War and after   European refugees
and Americans too   One ran into them here and there, on the
street (Isaac Stern coming out of the Rexall Drugstore in Beverly
Hills in his undershirt)   or at a concert (Igor Stravinsky
confiding to a younger composer, "J'aime vos mains")   Arnold

Schoenberg and George Gershwin played tennis together   Heifetz, Piatigorsky and Rubinstein played trios   Only slightly less renowned musicians provided the talent pool for the movie studios' orchestras

6.
There were exiled writers too   Brecht   Werfel   Thomas Mann   Adorno   Lion Feuchtwanger   I didn't know about them   I didn't know I was one of them   My parents found this futile paradise when I was small   They brought their books and their paintings and their language and their music to a place where only other exiles would recognize them   But they were happy in the seasonless sunshine   I was the displaced person, the inheritor of exile, the refugee who didn't know it   As the children of survivors are said to dream the nightmares of their parents, I inherited nameless fears   My parents wanted to forget   I dreamed of transcendence   My dreams made them afraid again   Their child was born on Kristallnacht, night of the shattered glass   Will her voice be heard?

smallpoems

1.
spread,
smoothed,
flattened
by the sun,

by love,

i am.

2.
I can't think why we should
(I wish you would)
be together
again.

3.
I remember those teeth
pushing through your kiss.

4.
My art so far has sprung
from my discontent

It could as well now arise
from my happiness

But happiness eludes me.

SNAKES DO IT

I've always wanted to know how snakes do it.
Make love, you know.
I mean, they seem all of a piece.
It's hard to imagine a protrusion or a hole.
I asked a vet from the zoo. He didn't seem to know,
just said, "they do it, don't worry,"
in a smart-ass, knowing way, as if to show
he was superior to my question.
I asked another vet, this one does research
on animal reproduction at a major New York hospital,
and he didn't seem to know either,
just muttered something about a cloaca.
I looked that up in the dictionary:
"The common chamber into which the intestinal,
urinary, and generative canals discharge."
Also a word for sewer.
He seemed to think that would satisfy me.
It didn't, of course. I was longing
to imagine the scene. Two snakes, you know.
Then while I was reading *Cosmo* at the gynecologist's
I came upon a fascinating article on love
in the animal world. Not only, it said,
not only does the male snake have a penis,
he has two penises. It seems one's a spare,
in case he loses one, or goes over a pothole, or something.
No wonder those guys didn't want to talk about it.

GHOSTS

Mitch, the doorman next door, has died.
He was retired, a Jewish marine.
He used to do odd jobs for me after
Peter left: sweep the steps, clear the
snow from the sidewalk, watch the house
when I was away. He died of cancer.

* * *

Peter was shot   He lived in the basement and took care of
the house   Mitch, who was his friend, said Peter was killed
as a result of his dealings in stolen goods   This may be true
     Peter was always bringing home presents from his "friend"
at Bloomingdale's   Dior robes, Gerber carving knives, a giant
ice bucket   He had already left me when he was killed   He
left after the baby was born because my husband couldn't get along
with him

Peter used to say he liked to play with people's brains   He
became angry at a lady he worked for and sent her a tombstone
     anonymously   Another lady received hundreds of dollars
worth of groceries she hadn't ordered, charged to her account
     He never did anything like that to us   He was quite
helpful   Told me, for instance, never to accept deliveries,
he would do it because he wouldn't have to tip   "Why not?"
I asked   "Do I look like Levine?" he said   He was Mexican-
Hawaiian

Peter liked to tell two stories about how we met   In one he
was standing outside Carnegie Hall begging, and we took pity on
him and brought him home   In the other, he was a poor orphan,
our tour guide in Mexico, and we liked him so much we took him
back to the U.S. with us

Peter loved my mother   "Our mother-in-law," he called her,
and the baby   "our baby"   His parting words were,
"There's too much love in this house"

* * *

Mark Rothko couldn't remember Peter's name.
He called him "Philip."
Peter, who cared for Mark, said,
"The next time he calls me 'Philip,'
I'm going to call him 'Mr. Motherwell.' "
He did, and it never happened again.

* * *

Rothko is dead. He was my friend.
He killed himself in his studio and didn't leave a note.
He lay in his blood on the kitchen floor, wrapped
in layers of underwear, water left running
in the sink. When the medical examiner had done,
I had to go and tell his wife. She was very calm.
Six months later she died of a cerebral hemorrhage.
People said he was murdered and that she committed suicide
but neither story was true. The same medical examiner came;
when she left I took their seven-year-old son
home with me and he and a neighborhood friend played
"dropping dead" in my basement all day, a stricken Peter
watching over them. I was pregnant with my own son then.

* * *

After David was born, after Mark died, and before Peter left,
Annette came to live with us   Annette was a French girl who

took care of my infant son   "Bonjour petit bébé joyeux,"
she would sing as she entered his room in the morning   "Good
morning joyous little baby"

Her father was a "marchand de truffes," a truffle merchant in
the Périgord   He often sent large tins of black truffles
which she shared with us   I learned to make truffle salad
     sliced truffles and celery marinated in a vigorous
vinaigrette   I also learned that if you put half a truffle
with eggs in a covered bowl for a few hours, the taste and scent
of truffle permeates the eggshells   Later your scrambled eggs
have a mysterious dark taste

Her own baby is dead   She asked me to arrange her abortion
     She ate spinach afterwards

I never saw Annette again after my husband discovered she was
a kleptomaniac   Apparently she stole things from stores, strangers,
and friends, although her friends loved her too much to report her
thefts to the police   They simply asked for their treasures
back and she complied, if she hadn't already sold them   "selective
lacunae," a psychiatrist friend called it   one little loophole
in her psyche, everything else in order   My husband found out
about it while I was away with the baby and fired her   I would
have kept her, I loved her   I believe she took very little from
us   There were a few unexplained disappearances   a pair
of new bikini underpants, one of three-for-five dollars I had
bought   a royal blue baby costume, a gift from Belgium   a
pair of inexpensive but much loved candlesticks   I turned the
house upside down looking for those   a rabbit fur coat I had
lent her, which she said was stolen from her at the movies

I've heard that she has a baby of her own now, and a husband

* * *

My father was a "marchand de diamants," a diamond merchant from Antwerp   He was born in Poland and grew up in Belgium   As a young man he traveled all over the world and learned to speak seven languages   He taught himself Spanish by attending the same movie twelve times in Mexico City   He died of something rare that mimicked cancer.

Sylvain was one of ten children   His father would come home from a business trip, pick up the nearest child, and say, "Hallo! Which little Poirier are you?"   I was his only child   To me he would say, "Go up to the bedroom and see if I'm there," when he wanted to be rid of me

He was resourceful and practical   When my mother declined an engagement ring, he gave her a Buick   With the Buick he was able to drive his family out of Belgium a day ahead of the German invasion of 1940   When he could no longer obtain gas, he deeded the car to a customs official in return for our unhindered crossing of a border   After standing in line all night outside the "sûreté" in Bayonne to obtain exit visas, my father saw the police commissioner kick out the first man in line   "How dare you try to bribe me with a thousand francs," he said   "Ten thousand," said Sylvain   "Come," said the official   Everyone my father knew in the crowd pressed their documents on him   "Take mine"   "Sylvain, take mine"   Once inside, he presented the passports   "Who are all these people?" the commissioner asked   "My aunt, my uncle, my brother, my cousin," replied my father   He got them all stamped

Once settled in America, he sold diamonds and played golf with
other Jewish eccentrics at the Hillcrest Country Club in Beverly
Hills   He ate an avocado every day and swam in his very own
kidney-shaped pool   He read the Book of Mormon for pleasure
even though he was a lifelong Zionist extremist   He had prospered
but wouldn't buy a Cadillac   too ostentatious, he said   He
liked a good bargain and he liked painting   Vlaminck   Utrillo
Picasso   Marie Laurencin   Daumier   He bought them at auction
    Sometimes they would be fakes   He didn't mind

* * *

Sylvain appreciated Rothko's painting as well.
I introduced him to Mark back in Belgium where both were visiting.
"There are some wonderful paintings here," said my father,
thinking of Rubens, Brueghel, even Delvaux.
Mark shrugged. ". . . not interested in painting," he said.
Later, thinking my father would be shocked,
I asked what he thought of Rothko.
". . . nice Jewish man," he shrugged.

* * *

This nice Jewish man was a painter who tried to take the color
out of his paintings   He was born in Russia but came directly
to America when he was young   He did not travel and learn
languages, and his outlook was not international, though he was
foreign, but also American   He had suffered no world wars,
and he felt out of place on his rare trips to Europe after his
late success

This artist's interest in other painters' work was limited
  He liked to know what the "competition" was doing, and
he was interested in how painters he admired achieved their
ends But he felt he had a statement to make, and this
statement was of a tragic and timeless nature Painting
was only the instrument with which he made the statement, and
color was only a part of the instrument He would have called
himself a prophet first and a painter second

He came to feel that viewers' appreciation of his vision was
being obscured by the attention given his colors that
people were being seduced by the colors and that their pleasure
was preventing them from making the further effort to understand
the subject of the work

So he tried to create works that were equal in meaning, but
with as little color as possible This was the raison-d'être
for the black and gray paintings, his very last to make
it impossible to bypass the message, so that those who had not
the interest or the courage to face the subject would not be
tempted to look at or to buy the paintings

"Go away," he seemed to be saying "Go away" And he
lay down one day with a razor blade among the dust-colored
paintings, and he waited for death to carry him away

PIANO LESSON

The cigarette lay on its side on the piano strings
just behind and to the left of the music rack.
It was lit, burning neatly,
the smoke rising at a right angle
as if supported by an unseen and very steady hand.

The cigarette had fallen out of my hand on its way to the ashtray
on top of a pile of music on the piano
which belonged to my teacher,
Herr Professor Julius Herford,
self-styled representative of J. S. Bach in Berlin.

Herford did not smoke. He did not approve of my smoking.
Neither did my father, who would have been enraged had he known.
I was nineteen.
The professor was threatening to inform my parents
if the piano were damaged.

We watched.
The cigarette burned slowly, independently,
leaving a perfectly shaped trail of ashes in its wake.
We wondered if the strings were being burned;
if we should try to retrieve the cigarette,
or if that would be even more dangerous.

Finally the filter tip met the fire
and the burning stopped.
The cigarette lay quietly on the strings, all passion extinguished,
the ashes forming an impeccable shadow substitute.
We did not dare to remove or even touch them.

I endured the suspense for several days,
waiting for word from the piano technician, via Julius Herford,
as to whether the strings had been damaged.
Finally the call came.
The piano was, miraculously, unhurt.

I think I paid the tuner's bill.

That summer Professor Herford came to visit my family in California
on his way to some festival or other in the region.
He did not tell my father that I smoked.
He did not tell him what a brilliant student I was.
He said that I had not paid for my last two lessons.

WORDS FOR THE POET

They fit in your poem like a pocket,
these sun-warmed shoes these spiny
spoons, in your poem like a pocket
empty cocoons in oval
rooms, they fit in your dream
like a poem, three green balloons two
seaweed spittoons one piebald
wound these words these choices
they fit in the pocket of your poem
like a dappled a daring ensnaring
despairing . . . bruise.

SOUP

The celery wasn't very tasty
and it was dirty. I washed it,
carefully, and dried it,
and cut it into small pieces.
That took a long time.
When it was cut up, diced, as they say,
it still looked a little dirty,
so I put the little pieces in a colander
and ran water over them again,
despite the fact that I would have to dry
all those little pieces once more,
and I was running out of paper towels as well.
I can't cook without paper towels.
It was for him, you see,
I was making the soup for him.
I love soup.

I heated some butter in my favorite black skillet
that cost only seven dollars years ago in France,
(I brought it back with me on a Norwegian freighter)
and which makes everything taste better,
and without which I'd be lost,
and dropped the celery in to soften in the butter.
Then I remembered the potato.
So I peeled it and washed it and diced it,
and put it in the pot with the celery and the butter.

Fifteen minutes later I had cleaned up the kitchen a little,
and stirred the vegetables around in the butter several times,
and they were doing nicely,
so I poured in ("moistened it with,"
as they say) some chicken broth and water,

and added salt and pepper
and a little of the dried thyme from France that I'm almost out of
(I'm lost without that too—
it makes everything taste better as well)
and let it simmer for a while.

I cleaned up a little more,
argued with my son David over his math homework,
square roots, which neither of us understands,
and read three articles in *The New York Times* while the soup cooked.
One was about Hitler's newly discovered diaries
which will probably turn out to be forgeries. . . .
I'm interested because of a psychobiography I once read
by Walter Langer, the first of its kind,
written during the war, long before any really personal details
about Hitler were known. Langer made the most amazing predictions
based on the most fragmentary data; for instance,
that Hitler would commit suicide under certain circumstances,
and that his preferred form of sex would involve being shat upon
by a woman. These things did turn out to be true.
The sexual prediction was later corroborated by former partners.
The second article was about financial aid to college students.
Should it be based more on merit than on need?
The third was about Betty Friedan winning a debate,
in the face of ridicule from Cambridge students,
on whether feminism was good for men.
She took the position that it was. I agreed.

By this time the celery was getting soft,
but the soup didn't taste too great.
It looked gray and murky, I thought,
like fog, but not like pea-soup which is green.

I'm very involved with this soup.
He, Bill, has often spoken of his fondness
(childish, I say) for canned celery soup.
I wanted to prove to him that fresh is better.
But now I was wondering if the companies that can soup
don't probably have access to better quality celery
than I do. Or maybe they use monosodium
glutamate, I don't know.
Anyway, I did know I had to improve the taste and color of This soup
or I wouldn't convince him of my love—
cooking can be an expression of love, don't you think?—
or of the souperiority of fresh food.

I let it cook a little more,
added some salt, and then took it off the fire,
and puréed it with my electric Soupmix from Belgium,
another essential ingredient in my culinary life.
Soupmix is a brand-name.
Now it was thicker and it tasted a little better too.
I put another lump of butter in it.
Then I looked in the fridge
and saw that I had three eggs.
Four would have been better.
I separated the yolks from the whites,
and put them in a bowl.
I whisked them hard. Added a few drops of lemon.
Whisked some more. Got some hot soup from the pot
and poured it slowly into the bowl,
whisking all the time.
Then I poured this mixture gently back into the pot,
and stirred for a while, over the flame,
until the soup thickened a little more.

I tasted it. Much better.
And it looked better too. The fog was clearing.
I added salt again. I thought awhile.
Then I offered my son a quarter
to go get me some heavy cream and parsley from Gristede's.
I had to explain about the two kinds of parsley
because I wanted the flat Italian kind, it has more flavor.
He returned with the cream and the curly kind.
He said he'd had to go to both Gristede's and Sloan's,
because at Gristede's they didn't know what flat parsley was,
and had told him, "Step on it, then it'll be flat."

I washed and chopped the parsley
and left it ready to put in at the last minute.
When Bill arrives I'll mix some cream
with warm soup and add that to the pot.
I hope it will be a good, nurturing,
convincing soup. One last problem:
Bill wants canned shrimp, the tiny ones,
in his soup. Another childhood whimsy,
I suppose. I've got the can, I bought it today.
Tiny Alaskan shrimp, two dollars and fifty-nine cents.
I was worried about pollution,
but I hoped Alaskan shrimp would be pure.
I was glad they weren't from Mexico
or Louisiana. Then David saw the can.
He added to my anxiety by insisting
that the can had a tiny dent in it
and that they had told him at school
you could get botulism that way.

I feel pretty good about the soup now,
but I'm worried about the shrimp.
I won't open the can till Bill gets home.
Maybe he'll change his mind about putting shrimp in his soup,
though he's not one to worry. Botulism and pollution
are not his particular bugaboos.
This soup is only for Bill and me, by the way.
David hates celery and Maureen can't have salt
because of her high blood pressure.
It's a good thing no one cares about cholesterol.
All those eggs, all that cream and butter.

* * *

Well, the soup was great.
The cream and the eggs gave it body and character.
Bill put the shrimp in his, and loved it.
And he was still alive the next morning.
There was another surprise too. David tasted some of Bill's soup
(with shrimp) and liked it, and even ate some
because, he said, it didn't taste like celery.
It didn't look like celery either.
Next time, I'll ask Bill to go to Spagnoli's
and get fresh shrimp. If they have the tiny kind,
that is. They have to be tiny.
And I'll ask him to buy them cooked.
I don't like cooking shrimp,
it's not interesting like making soup,
and they smell bad while they're cooking.
But at least David and I won't have to worry about botulism.
And maybe Mr. Spagnoli will know about which waters are polluted.

* * *

I've just read all this aloud to David.
He says it's the only poem he's ever read
that's also a recipe. He says,
you could probably make soup from this poem.
Since he's brought that truth to my attention,
I'd better tell you that I forgot to say
I put in a chopped onion as well to soften with the celery and the potato
at the very beginning of this soup-poem.
I think it's important to be honest.

II

SINGLES

There are one point nine six persons
in each household in Manhattan
which means that over half
of the seven hundred and four thousand
occupied units in Manhattan
have only one person living in them

this is the lowest number of persons
per household in any county in the whole
United States of America   with one
exception

and that exception is a county in Hawaii
which has one point four six persons
per household

and that county in Hawaii is a leper colony.

NIGHT'S BODIES

"I sleep to escape my life,
arise to still my dreams. . . ."

* * *

I am suffering from amusia,
the inability to produce musical sounds,
the loss of ability to make music.
The condition is desperate,
potentially fatal,
I know.

* * *

I travel to France
to have the left hand joined
to the right at the wrist.
Surgery is required
to reinforce GROWTH and stability.
But the surgeons understand
BROKEN stability
and refuse to perform the operation.

* * *

What do I know about trills?
    that they should be practiced slowly
    and played evenly   sometimes
    it helps to accent the first note
    or to start slowly and then speed up

        . . . practicing trivializes

* * *

A friend confides that he is unable to quiet his inner voices.
I advise him never to lift his thumbs from the keys,
to press down on the note itself,
instead of striking from above.

* * *

>She lies, Nō-painted, between us
>   We are helping her to die
>   I am kind, but I cringe
>   when she touches me
>   She is a vision, white-masked, of myself
>   He says we are killing her
>   She will no longer come between us
>   "But I am kind!" I cry
>   You are, he says   Always

* * *

The telephone rings in the middle of the night.
I am frightened out of deep sleep.
An unknown man's voice asks if I am Anne-Marie.
"Do you put polish on your toenails?" he asks
"What?" I gasp   "Do you?" he purrs

I dream that my legs are encased in primeval slime.
I am Anne-Marie.

TELEGRAM

ON A STEPLADDER WATERING THE TALL PLANTS XMAS NIGHT   STOP   XMAS NIGHT I HAPPENED TO LOOK DOWN AT THE STREET   STOP   UNDER ONE OF THE NEW SODIUM LAMPS I THOUGHT I SAW A WOMAN   STOP   A WOMAN AND A MAN IN A PARKED CAR   STOP   WHAT THE HELL I WONDERED WHAT THE HELL WERE THEY DOING ON XMAS NIGHT IN A PARKED CAR ON AN EMPTY STREET UNDER A STREET LAMP IT WASN'T SAFE   STOP   I LOOKED HARDER   STOP   HARDER SHE WAS BENT OVER EATING   STOP   HIM   EATING HIM   STOP   I FINISHED WATERING THE PLANTS AND LOOKED DOWN AT THE STREET AGAIN   STOP   STILL THERE   STOP   STILL THERE SHE ROLLED DOWN THE WINDOW AND SPAT   STOP   SHE SPAT SHE SPAT   STOP.

FROM NEW YORK

HOIST WITH HER OWN PETARD

She made a great beautiful chocolate penis. She made it and he photographed it and she sent it to a great beautiful literary magazine. She sent it in the hope that they would publish it. At the time that she made this penis, she gave him a recipe for gingerbread cake. He baked the gingerbread cake and he submitted it to the same literary magazine with the same hope. After a long wait the editors accepted his cake and they rejected her penis. She was indignant. She was especially indignant since it was she who had given him the gingerbread recipe in the first place. She demanded to know why they had rejected her chocolate penis when they had accepted his gingerbread cake. "It was much too large," the editors said. "No way could we run anything that large." She imagined it running off the edge of the page. But her chocolate penis wasn't that large, she realized, it wasn't too large for publication at all. It was his 8 by 10 glossy that made it look too large.

RETURN TO THE POEM

OK for a girl to be out on the steps
in her robe and gown and slippers
on a January night, comfortable,
the air not harsh enough to send her back inside
before her curiosity has waned

Strange to be on a Manhattan street
in her nightshirt and L L Bean Slippersox
at one in the morning,
drawn by the smell of cooking smoke
and watching the fire trucks across the street

Strange to be doing that
but all right because the steps are hers,
no one will stare,
the police won't pick her up for loitering
on the street in her nightclothes

She's watching from her own steps
so the perimeters of OK are extended
a little farther for her, this night . . .
And glad that the fire is across the street
and that there are so many fire engines

And knowing where the smoke comes from
and that the fire is being cared for,
she loses interest and turns inside,
back to the poem she has left on the table,
and considers if her poem does not lie . . .

TWO-PART INVENTION

1.

"What's so great about men?" he asked. "We-ell, you've got that great thing between your legs," she ventured. "Ah, you can buy those in the drugstore," he scoffed. The elevator stopped, the door opened. In a few seconds they were on the street. The question lay unresolved.

Another time, watching him upon his return from a long trip, she wondered: if it turned out that he'd lost his penis, would she still love him. This question, also, lay unresolved.

2.

An electric heater throwing its light across the dark room,
a blanket spread upon the floor,
two pillows.

These were his preparations for her arrival.

Later, their bodies locked in amorous combat,
"Doucement," she said.
"Too small?" he heard.

Ah no, not that.

The next day
the bruised bones of her pelvis sang to her of the spare boards
of his floor.

"You are like a monk who loves women," she told him.

3.

"I feel as though I'm farting into your music," he said, whacking away at his Stockhausen on one side of the rehearsal hall while she played Chopin on the Pleyel at the other side. They continued to practice, back to back, each aware of the other and sometimes listening, but disturbing each other not at all.

4.

He made love energetically, using his fingers the way he used them to play the piano. Not caressingly but percussively. This did not preclude tenderness. But it was an abstract tenderness, totally without sentiment.

5.

His face was intelligent, unique, and magnetically attractive. Both men and women were drawn to his beauty and basked in his warmth until they discovered that this beautiful god was available to them only so long as they remained strangers; they became his enemies then. He said his dream of a woman was a beautiful stranger, not to know or be known by, and his life was a procession of thus encapsulated encounters all over the world. His satisfaction in the "romance" of parting left scores of women with a more affirmative view of love, or life, hungry for more, desolate or vengeful. Sometimes they would tell his wife.

6.

"But is happiness everything?" he asked, trying to leave her.

"No-o," she mused, "but it's not nothing."

7.

It was Christmas,
snow covering the ground,
his body covering hers,
sound of white peace, quiet
joy like an Invention by Bach.
It's heaven, he said,
I know, said she,
You can't know, said he,
because you're you
and I'm only me.

8.

She comes across a sentence in a book: "Typical of the marriages of writers of genius (and other artists) is the intensely creative woman artist who loves the neurotic, possibly psychotic man; she cannot live without him, he is her secret Muse, bringing her poetry—and at the same time tearing her life apart."

9.

"You need him for your physical well-being," suggested Tibor the astrologer. She nodded vigorously. It was exciting to have her unacknowledged feelings given shape by a stranger.

"He enhances your creativity, he doesn't take from you."

Yes, yes.

"You are good for each other. So what is wrong?"

"He's afraid," she says. "He pushes me away all the time."

"He is right. He is a man of honor. Such a man would find it difficult to change."

She is incredulous. *"What shall I do?"*

"You are very demanding. Women are always at fault in these matters."

She muzzles her outrage. "All right. Will somebody else come into my life?"

"Do not abandon him for another!" came the reply, a commandment from on high.

Resentful and reassured, she prepared to leave.

"Wait!" Jupiter aimed a bolt of lightning. "He may well outsmart you."

10.

"Can you imagine," he once said, "that someone would say such a thing about me, that I'm like a cow who gives the most beautiful milk—and then kicks over the bucket!"

"Extraordinary," she nodded.

11.

Food. It was perhaps a bad sign that he wasn't interested in food. He cared only about not eating what was not supposed to be good for one. Tea yes, coffee no. Vitamins yes. Sugar no. The way to his heart was definitely not through his stomach. On the contrary, it sometimes seemed that his approach to her was that of a chronic dieter to much-beloved chocolate cake. Since she represented the ultimate sensual pleasure, she was tasteable without guilt only once in a while. Two days in a row was cause for remorse and a whole night, not to mention a week of her company caused indigestion, palpitations, and vows to reform and not partake again—maybe never again—of chocolate cake.

12.

". . . if you don't want me . . ." she said.

"Don't you know I always don't want what I want!" he responded with great irritation.

"Oh my god," she thought desperately.

"I must leave you, I must," he muttered, pacing the floor. "But the next time I come to your door," he begged, turning to face her, "please throw me out."

13.

"Are you a man or a mouse?" she demanded.

"I'm a mouse-ochist," he grinned, and changed the subject.

14.

She finds another passage in a book: "They admire and they desire purposeless death in the shape of self-sacrifice. . . . It is their deepest longing. The French or the British want victory; Germans always only want to die."

15.

From one of the many letters of farewell she has received from him: ". . . my respect for you and for me demands exactly what you think it forbids: a huge sacrifice, perhaps not a final one."

YOURS

You make me feel not
unwanted   but like Circe
I do not lure you

to your death but to
your life   by imagining
that I will make you

my victim
you make me

yours.

EUPHORBIA
(an herbal account)

I am suffering from euphorbia
which is the opposite of feverfew.
I have been given horehound and hyssop
and placed on mellow maltese crosses
which have in turn been placed on
our lady's bedstraw to rest.
Teasel and tansy dance a rocambole around me
in order to speedwell my recovery
and to make me comfrey.
I am annointed with beebalm and glory,
clary and bugle are sounded so that
the roman wormwood which galls me
may not borage farther into my
already fragrant and decorative body.

In the shadows sweet cicely and sweet woodruff,
epicures both, wait with nepeta cataria, ready
to germander my lovage should I
fall prey to the euphorbia
which has me.

I am a long root.

BROWN STUDY

I climb the stairs to your loft.
You open to me with a cold desirous stare
which frightens me.
You show me your toys   musical instruments,
clappers, mallets, drums   electronic equipment.
Rehearsal city, you say.
You show me your room, your bed.
Everything is brown.
You give me tea.
You play the music you have written.

I am a guest in a large brown room
inhabited by a composer
who uses rhythmic and harmonic repetitions
in which minute variations are barely apparent
to draw people irresistibly into his sphere. . . .
I do not wish to be drawn unknowing
into this droning

We lie on your bed.
Your music surrounds us.
You nudge me with your soft beard.
I tell you I have my period.
You shrug.
The music, obsessive, insists.
I shrug.

We rise. The brown bed is red.
Like a battlefield, I think, sourly,
With pride.

NOVENA

I was happy once for nine days.
My housekeeper found a novena for hopeless cases
on her seat in church,
a prayer to be recited every day for nine days,
and she thought she might as well say it for me
since I had been complaining of hard times.
She apologized for calling me a hopeless case
when she told me about it,
but I said I would accept help in any form.

During those nine days
my relations with a lover went very well,
I thought, too well as it turned out.
I gave an inspired performance of a great piano concerto in Texas.
And the first morning in the hotel, when the toilet wouldn't flush
after I had filled it with fecal matter and menstrual blood,
the gentle Mexican man with impeccable manners
to whom I apologized when he came up to fix it
said don't worry, no problem, have a nice day.

I wore a green and purple dress to the concert
and no one criticized my attire or my playing.
Indeed they said the colors of my dress were spiritual,
that I created sounds of such power and beauty that I cast
a hypnotic spell over the audience. It was a love affair—
with the orchestra, the conductor, the critics. With my lover too,
as long as I stayed away. But when I returned he fled,
saying he'd been having too many erotic dreams about me,
I was becoming an addiction, he couldn't handle it.
That was the tenth day.

So then things went back to normal.
The critics wrote about my hair, did it hide my face,
was it too long; they criticized my clothes,
said there were too many women on that year's subscription list,
blamed my playing for Chopin's skimpy orchestration.
The men in my life were skittery again.
I wanted Maureen to say the novena again,
but she said she couldn't, because after nine days of happiness,
I wasn't a hopeless case anymore.

III

NUN OF MY DREAMS

1.
Instead of going to a movie last night
we took the bus to Rizzoli on 57th Street
and bought Michelin maps of France and Paris
and a tiny French/English dictionary.
I had to pee so we checked out the facilities
at Donald Trump's Tower across Fifth Avenue—
very nice gift to the city, Donald—
and then on to the Oak Room at the Plaza
where they get five dollars for a glass of wine.
I wanted to lose three pounds
so I could do some serious eating in France,
but I went off my diet at the Plaza
what with the atmosphere and free peanuts
and all. I had meant to have a Perrier
which I loathe, but I had white wine instead,
and then I couldn't sleep, so I read Waverly Root
on the food and history of the Loire Valley,
one of the places we're going, and that reminded me
how anti-semitic history is—
the Jews of the town were all burned alive
at Chinon in 1321. What do I want
with their old châteaux anyway. What I really want
is one very particular little château, a hotel
in its own park on the banks of the Indre,
and a wine, Saint-Nicolas-de-Bourgueil—
that doesn't travel, as they say—and that I want
to drink again. Well, I've been to Madrid
and not gone to the Prado, I can pass over
the châteaux with histories I don't cotton to.
We'll just make love in their shadows, picnic
and frolic on the river banks, and so on.

2.
I'm going with Bill. He says he'll be my chauffeur,
but I have a different idea because of a dream
I had, living alone, before I met him,
about having a party and being tipped off
that my house was going to be burglarized
that very night. The locks had been tampered with
so it would be easier for the burglars to enter
when the time came. I didn't know
what to do, it was evening already,
I had this party going on in my house,
and it was with the utmost feeling of relief
that I realized the solution to my problem
was to call an all-night locksmith to fix the locks.
So simple, why hadn't I thought of it before?
There was a nun in the dream, a Belgian nun,
guest at the party, who looked something like me.
She was standing in the library, proudly
showing everyone a letter she had written.
I wondered if it were all right for a nun
to be so self-congratulatory. I was a pianist
at the time so it was hard to imagine myself
as the nun. I told my friend Bob about the dream
and asked what he thought it meant.
"It means you want an all-night locksmith,"
he snickered.

3.
The all-night locksmith and I
are going to be in Paris for a couple of days as well,
but they're the wrong days for food and museums.
Chez Maître Paul is closed, and so is Fauchon

where I like to buy my dried thyme from Provence,
and Victor Hugo's house, where I like to look
at the drawings and think about his crazy daughter.
Jo Goldenberg's is always open though,
and I think it will be good for Bill,
who's Irish/Alsatian from the Midwest,
and not a Francophile that he's aware of,
to have his first meal in Paris at a French
Kosher Yiddish pub. He's been to Paris before, of course,
but only to work, photographing de Gaulle and that,
not to hang out. We can go to the Jew de Paume
(Whoops, Freudian typos are wild, that's "Jeu")
and the Beaubourg—sublime to the ridiculous—
I don't mean the contents of course, just the buildings.

4.
Speaking of the contents, I had another dream
in which a painting by Vlaminck was stolen
from my parents' house in Beverly Hills.
I didn't understand the dream at all
until I realized that the painting was of three nuns
walking away, down a path, from a church or convent.
So that here was another nun-burglary dream.
I grew up with that painting. My mother sold it
after my father died. Sometime later I saw it displayed
in the drawing room of the dealer who had bought it.
I was surprised and asked if he had decided to keep it.
But he said that it had been very difficult to resell
because only Jewish people bought Vlamincks in this country,
and they wouldn't buy a picture of nuns and a convent.

5.
He said he might send it to Belgium to sell.
We'll go there too.
I want to show Bill a convent in Bruges,
the Béguinage, where the lay nuns used to make lace.
I flew there once to play a concert.
When I arrived, I realized I'd forgotten
to bring the music I was to play.
I called my mother to send it to me.
While I was waiting, I dreamt that she had sent a packet
of my stream-of-consciousness scribblings instead.
I'd better concentrate on food—tiny fresh shrimp
and the best "frites" in the world.
And history—the house I was born in,
the one where my mother was raised.
And love—I do.
And keep a record of the entire trip,
all I do and say and dream,
and suck poems from those memories,
and grow plump and smiling and pleased,
standing like a nun in the library of my dreams.

VARIATIONS

She was divorced
with five children.
Her husband had remarried.
Each summer he would take their kids
and his new ones on a driving trip.
Each summer he would have a catastrophic
accident in which one or more children,
his or theirs, were killed or injured.

Her psychiatrist said,
"He is trying to kill all his children."
But they could never be sure.
It could never be proved
that the accidents were his fault,
and she could never get a court order
forbidding him to take her children
on automobile trips.

She was my dearest friend
until my husband and I separated. Then
she began taking his part in small matters.
I learned that she had been repeating
distorted versions of things I had said
about him. She had made him feel I was glad
to be rid of him. Perhaps it was true.
I never spoke to her again.

After our separation
my husband became angry and resentful
and I became fearful
when he took our children driving,
though I never said anything.

Years later, feeling my unwillingness
to let them go with him he said,
"I'm not like her husband, you know."
He knew.

He died soon after, of natural causes.
She hugged me at his funeral.
They must have been lovers.
I'm not afraid anymore.

SAD ABOUT CORA DuBOIS

Cora DuBois, Harvard Professor of Anthropology, Is Dead at 87
(obituary, *The New York Times*, April 11, 1991)

There were only two women on the faculty at Harvard in those days
and they were both full professors.
The other one's name was Cecilia Payne-Gaposchkin
and she was an astronomer.
I didn't know her—
one was proud merely to be able to pronounce her name.

I remember those two,
their existence as the solitary female professors,
though I remember no sense of outrage at the fact.
That was the late nineteen-fifties.

I did know Cora DuBois.
I remember being received at her home
with my anthropology grad-student boyfriend,
and being told she lived with a companion,
named in today's obituary,
and being somewhat in awe,
and understanding that this was a homosexual relationship,
and accepting that as well.

In the fifties
we accepted everything as presented.

A little later   the early sixties, perhaps,
Harvard did begin to hire women   at the instructor level,
which was about the level of a maintenance engineer,
but they rarely promoted these women,

and never to tenure like Cora and Cecilia.
How did those two manage it?

And there was always a flap
about how they couldn't hire women
because there were no bathrooms for them,
the Faculty Club being a male bastion anyhow.
I think women were allowed inside only as guests at lunch
to eat the horsemeat steak.
Did they make exceptions for Cora and Cecilia?

We were proud of them,
but we didn't understand.
We were the ones who wouldn't be hired,
the other women.

Wellesley

I was a student at an all-girls' college nearby,
Wellesley College, Wellesley, Mass.
We did have women professors   and men too
and we accepted that as well.
I guess the thinking was that women could teach boys
as their mothers
but not as their professors
but they could teach girls as both.

Well, at Wellesley you weren't allowed to leave the premises
after 10 p.m. If you had a late date you had to wait ouside
in the freezing cold. You weren't allowed to have a car until
your senior year, even though that meant you were stuck out there
in the middle of nowhere. Or maybe that was the point.

You could have a man in your room only on Sunday afternoons
from three to five with the door three inches ajar.
And when your male guest arrived in the lobby
the student slave on "bells" would shout to the entire dorm
over the speaker system, "Man on Five!"

Once the Man was Tarzan.
I remember, because Buster Crabbe's daughter lived on my floor.
He was Tarzan in the movies then.

You were summarily expelled for sexual activity of any kind.
One year a group of girls who liked each other
were found to have been having some sort of relations
with each other, in my dorm.
They were all expelled.
Another time a girl was found to have been sleeping
with a Harvard graduate student.
She was expelled.
He was only reprimanded.
He finished graduate school and went on
to a distinguished career in academia.
She got married.

We were fed a disastrous diet of fats and carbohydrates,
our vitamin C and calcium intake severely restricted.
We were allowed only one glass of milk a day.
Our gums bled and we gained weight, while the Harvard boys
filled their trays gleefully, again and again,
telling us over and over, "We can have all we want!"

We were forced to do all kinds of KP and other duties:
bus, waitressing at dinner, serving behind the counter
at breakfast and lunch, operating the switchboard.
It was supposed to be good for our character.
The boys did nothing.
I remember standing behind the counter where I was supposed
to be serving fried eggs at breakfast one morning,
and fainting while a girl named Anneliese changed her mind
over and over,
about which fried egg she wanted me to put on her plate.

We were underfed,
forced to work without compensation
(our parents paid for this)
denied sex or alcohol
(you were expelled for drinking also)
our ability to leave the premises severely curtailed.
Even more serious—
it was made extremely difficult
for us to receive a grade of "A."
I was told by my freshman philosophy professor
that my paper would have to be publishable
in a professional journal
for me to receive an "A."
My male friends at Harvard got "A's" quite easily
and passed without trouble into graduate school.
They had better grade averages.

Who would believe it now?
Who could have had such a college experience?
Only Anne-Marie would write this.

M. H.

Still,
I feel sad about Cora DuBois.
My boyfriend, who became my husband,
would have been upset as well.
We're divorced now, and he's dead too,
but I feel he would have called me this morning
on reading the obituary,
and we would have shared our memories,
our shared memories of her and of those days.
He would have called.
Partly, I feel bad for him.
I mean, I feel bad he's not here to know that she died.
Is that dumb?
I feel that way whenever something that would have touched him
comes my way—a great performance, a nice bit of gossip.
"Never trust a person who does not have a banal streak,"
he used to say.
I feel bad he's not here to feel bad with me.
And to reminisce.
I have no one to share my memories.
Or is it our past I grieve for?

A TOE FANTASY

1. Moses supposes his toeses are roses. Moses supposes erroneously. But Moses supposes his toeses are roses—that's what Moses supposes his toeses to be.

2. Aaron, nine years old, telephones his friend Ike and declares that he dialed the number with his big toe. He has a push-button toe. I mean phone.

3. Mira, who did something unknowable to Ike in a park which resulted in his being instantly toilet trained, goes to visit her family on their farm in Brittany. Her chief pleasures there have always been manly ones—driving the tractor and harvesting the cauliflower in winter. One day she hefts the power mower over her toes and returns to Isaac minus the two smallest ones on her right foot.

4. Mira's godmother has cancer. She is persuaded that she got it because many years ago, when a girl in France, a doctor attached a tiny piece of radium to her big toe for three weeks to cure a wart. Now she has a wart in her breast.

5. Isaac's mother Sarah and her friend Flora formed a "dextrous toes" club when they were adolescents as a result of Sarah's accidentally breaking her little finger when she sat on it in a fit of hysterical teenage laughter. She and Flora delighted in picking various objects off the floor with toes which spread and curled, and were possessed of a fingerlike articulation and independence of movement.

6. Which ability to spread and act independently has aroused Sarah's lover Abe to a fierce and previously unawakened competitive zeal. He practices spreading his toes now with the same fine spirit with which he jumps his rope and pursues his Sarah.

7. This lover dreamt that there was a blister-white ring around his big toe. And that it turned to blood as the toe fell off.

8. The lay psychologist who was not consulted about this dream is the podiatrist who used to trim Sarah's ingrown toenails. One day his secretary revealed that on the other side of the door he had a separate and independent practice in psychology. Neither set of clients knew about the other.

9. This podiatrist worked with diabetics who have problems with their toes. Flora's fiancé is a diabetic and has lost his big toe to gangrene.

10. It is said that Saint Francis Xavier lost his big toe to a nun who bit it off for a keepsake, and that an Indian man sacrificed one of his to an electric fan which wriggled five feet toward him and chopped it off as he slept.

11. Sometimes fantasies come true.

FRIENDS

We were friends, the poet and I.
He helped me with my poems.
He took an interest in my life, my love,
my child. Our dogs were friends.

He lived with a friendly and hospitable girl,
but she left him for a younger man
with whom she could have children.
He was lonely.

I introduced him to some of my friends.
Soon he met a woman he would marry.
He came to visit and talked about their meeting.
He presented her to me at a party.
There was no time for conversation.

Months later we collided, he and I,
in a small hotel in Paris.
He seemed glad to see me but embarrassed.
He couldn't say how long he had been there.
Then his wife came.

Perhaps they were on their honeymoon.
She said hello, eyes lowered, and walked out the door.
He looked embarrassed again.
Suddenly he said good-bye and walked out too.

Later that evening Bill and I knocked at their door.
She wouldn't let us in.
"What do you want?" she called through the door.
"We-have-nothing-to-say-to-you."

And my friend, the poet,
who had helped me with my poems,
wouldn't come to the door and wouldn't speak to us.
His new wife spoke for him.

AUTOBIOGRAPHICAL POETRY

I feel terrible,
aching muscles, exhaustion,
I look terrible,
pasty skin, long hair suddenly limp,
wrong haircut,
I've got a virus, upper respiratory,
something invisible I can't shrug off,
and an eye allergy that robs my eyes of their hooded lids,
my asymmetrical face of its desperate balance.
I wish for a hood to cover me,
Freud was born with a caul.

I drag myself too often to those whose work it is
to calm those devastations of the surface
which are, like coincidences,
the visible traces of untraceable principles.
A physicist said that, not a medium.
I have even visited my lover's confessor.
We live in a fast-food culture, she said,
You should be more patient.
Your moods have a bad effect on other people,
Civilize those discontents.
Afterwards I dreamt that my father
sent a psychic cat to eat my mother.
I knew about it and didn't stop it.
The guilt was terrible.
We still had the cat. Would it eat me?
And so on. I didn't go back.

I went to a stockbroker and bought a little IBM
for my son, for the future,

and promised myself to add some AT&T
even though I felt I shouldn't buy stock
in a company that was fucking us over.
But then why not, I thought,
We can re-coup by making money from the profits they will earn
by fucking us over,
and that kind of thinking was making me feel all twisted and deformed
like one of the pencils handed out at Christmas
by the Ukrainian chiropractor I had visited,
a weightlifter with an overdeveloped neck
who seemed foreshortened, like peasants in the paintings of a Russian
primitive named Burliuk. He had lifts in his shoes,
dandruff in his pants cuffs, and his crippled pencils were inscribed,
"Help! I need a chiropractor."

(I need a choreographer. Or a confidante.
I've been listening to him for weeks.
Finally he asks about me. "If it's too bad though,
don't tell me," he says.)

Some music then. Chopin Nocturnes perhaps.
Something cool, melancholy, without struggle.
Or some Bach, music of celebration,
not Beethoven—that's expression.
You object. "But the celestial last, or the late . . . "
No. Think of the German Expressionist painters;
Ludwig could have been one of them.
He wrote about himself, his music is not soothing
(this poem is not soothing)
it is expression, it won't bring you peace,
it is earthbound, inside the struggle,
not above it.

I still feel terrible.
And now China has proposed to Germany and Switzerland
that she store their radioactive wastes
in return for the Western currency she so badly needs.
Liberals feel it is evil to tempt a country
with economic problems more severe than our own
to become a dump for our toxic garbage.
But I imagine a scenario in which China
stores our nuclear wastes in her Gobi desert,
free from the care of possible damage
to her civilian population,
all the while becoming rich on our payments.
Eventually she is able to extract from our spent fuel
enough plutonium to make more nuclear weapons,
and emerges with money and bombs enough
to rule the world, or destroy it.

I went to a poetry reading. Two poets
had been asked to read autobiographical poems.
One said he didn't write them,
the other that he had thought everything one wrote was.
So they read what they pleased, from outside the struggle.
Edmond Jabès says speaking about oneself
always embarrasses poetry.
What do you think?
Yes.
But then, poetry can take care of itself.
And—is it poetry that's embarrassed
or is it oneself?
And—embarrassment isn't the worst thing
that can happen to a poem.

Should I confront the issue?   At least
I won't be caught unprepared if anyone asks me
for an autobiographical poem.

COLOPHON

This book was set in Schneidler, printed on acid-free Mohawk Superfine paper, and bound with a Strathmore wrapper.

Eight hundred and fifty copies were printed for a paper edition with a frontispiece by Elise Asher, "Moondial," 1987-88.

One hundred and fifty copies were hardbound with the frontispiece hand-colored by the artist.

The hardbound copies are numbered, titled, and signed by the author and the artist.